Toward a New Paradigm of Sustainable Development

Lessons from the Partnership for Growth

Author
JERI JENSEN

A Report of the CSIS Project on U.S. Leadership in Development

SEPTEMBER 2013

CSIS | CENTER FOR STRATEGIC &
INTERNATIONAL STUDIES

ROWMAN & LITTLEFIELD
Lanham • Boulder • New York • Toronto • Plymouth, UK

About CSIS

For 50 years, the Center for Strategic and International Studies (CSIS) has developed solutions to the world's greatest policy challenges. As we celebrate this milestone, CSIS scholars are developing strategic insights and bipartisan policy solutions to help decisionmakers chart a course toward a better world.

CSIS is a nonprofit organization headquartered in Washington, D.C. The Center's 220 full-time staff and large network of affiliated scholars conduct research and analysis and develop policy initiatives that look into the future and anticipate change.

Founded at the height of the Cold War by David M. Abshire and Admiral Arleigh Burke, CSIS was dedicated to finding ways to sustain American prominence and prosperity as a force for good in the world. Since 1962, CSIS has become one of the world's preeminent international institutions focused on defense and security; regional stability; and transnational challenges ranging from energy and climate to global health and economic integration.

Former U.S. senator Sam Nunn has chaired the CSIS Board of Trustees since 1999. Former deputy secretary of defense John J. Hamre became the Center's president and chief executive officer in April 2000.

About the Project

The Project on U.S. Leadership in Development is a partnership with Chevron Corporation focused on leveraging all U.S. assets—the private sector in particular—to promote economic development, improve livelihoods, and reduce poverty worldwide. The project seeks to renew the discourse in Washington and develop a fresh, actionable set of policy recommendations. The project builds on the ongoing work of CSIS in demography, economic development, global health, water and food security, trade, and governance.

ISBN 978-1-4422-2773-6 (pb); 978-1-4422-2774-3 (eBook)
Library of Congress Cataloging-in-Publication Data
CIP information available upon request.

Center for Strategic and International Studies
1800 K Street, NW, Washington, DC 20006
202-887-0200 | www.csis.org

Rowman & Littlefield
4501 Forbes Boulevard, Lanham, MD 20706
301-459-3366 | www.rowman.com

Contents

EXECUTIVE SUMMARY

The Obama administration has the opportunity to achieve more sustainable development solutions with a new model of development relevant in a world where private investment is the primary driver of economic growth.

Rather than trying to tackle the various structural barriers that limit the achievement of this vision through organizational changes that are unlikely in the near term, this paper examines a more direct route to sustainable development outcomes[1] for the U.S. government.

This approach is less about interagency architecture, and more about flexible and enthusiastic application of existing tools to spur new investment by lowering the risks and costs of investment with developmental impact. It suggests an approach that uses U.S. government resources and tools to attract, rather than to displace or ignore, private capital, and sees U.S. development agencies as the catalytic minority shareholders in development they have become.

This development model recognizes that sustainable growth cannot be achieved without attracting and engaging non-aid partners, that is, nongovernmental participants in development that includes the private sector, in particular, the core business of investors. Indeed, for more than a decade, developing countries have attracted more foreign direct investment[2] than development assistance.[3]

This new model fully embraces the U.S. government as a supporting actor in development, sharing an interest with investors in lowering the risk of sustainable investment and creating an enabling environment for economic growth. It does this by providing the processes, incentives, and tools to attract socially impactful investment around development priorities.

---

1. For purposes of this paper, sustainable development is defined as development projects that directly stimulate the creation of new jobs, businesses, and skills by attracting investment to development priorities.

2. For purposes of this paper, investment is defined as outward foreign direct investment.

3. Since 1980–1985, when outward foreign direct investment averaged $50 billion a year, the magnitude has grown by a factor of 40 to surpass $2.1 trillion in 2007, now leveling out to an average of $1.1 trillion post-financial crisis. See World Bank, *2012 World Development Indicators* (Washington, DC: World Bank, 2012), http://data.worldbank.org/sites/default/files/wdi-2012-ebook.pdf. In Africa, foreign direct investment projects have grown at a compound rate of 22 percent annually since 2007, well beyond development assistance from donors, which has remained essentially flat. See Ernst and Young, "Africa 2013," May, 2013, http://www.ey.com/Publication/vwLUAssets/The_Africa_Attractiveness_Survey_2013/$FILE/Africa_Attractiveness_Survey_2013_AU1582.pdf. Over the last 50 years, private foreign investment has replaced foreign aid as the principal source of funding for international economic development. See Carol Adelman, Kacie Marano, and Yulya Spantchak, *The Index of Global Philanthropy and Remittances 2012* (Washington, DC: Hudson Institute, 2012), http://www.hudson.org/files/publications/2012IndexofGlobalPhilanthropyand Remittances.pdf; and U.S. Agency for International Development, "Public Private Partnerships: Doing Business through Partnership," http://ec.europa.eu/europeaid/infopoint/documents/presentations/presentation_25_05_2010_en.pdf.

It is an approach that leads with the interests of the investors the U.S. and other governments are trying to attract to sustainable projects to achieve development goals. It suggests finally recognizing the U.S. government in a supporting role and the private sector, rather than governments, as the primary drivers of development.

That was a key objective of the Obama administration in its U.S. Global Development Policy of 2010. The Presidential Policy Directive (PPD) states the United States will "reorient its approach [to development] to prioritize partnership with private actors from policy conception through implementation, finding new ways to leverage our investments and to spur the action of others in Washington and the field."

The directive also states that in order to ensure effective implementation of the new policy, the United States will "generate greater coherence across the U.S. government," and that the National Security Council (NSC) "will coordinate development policy across the executive branch."[4] Since then, the administration has launched a continuum of initiatives to implement this vision, including Feed the Future, Grow Africa, Power Africa,[5] and the Partnership for Growth (PfG) initiative.

PfG is one of the first experiments to operationalize the administration's Global Development Strategy to bring greater programmatic coherence to U.S. trade and development initiatives in four countries—the Philippines, El Salvador, Ghana, and Tanzania—in Washington and on the ground.

A key goal was to reinforce a country-led approach, but to also bring to the development table the considerably deeper pockets of non-aid actors, as well as what they are best at bringing—the jobs, training, new businesses, domestic supply chain, and market linkages that are the fundamental ingredients of any sustainable development strategy.

Informal conversations with more than 30 U.S. government officials involved in PfG, and interested representatives from the private sector, nongovernmental community and other development stakeholders,[6] suggest the PfG process has helped to move the U.S. government some distance toward more coordinated and sustainable development solutions.

For example, greater U.S. government agency coordination has resulted through shared analyses of constraints to investment in PfG countries, which, for the first time, has provided a map for strategic coordination in four countries, at least in Washington.

Greater National Security Staff (NSS) involvement in U.S. trade and development strategy has resulted in better alignment between USAID and Millennium Challenge Corporation (MCC) programs[7] in these four countries—no small feat, considering that these two agencies represent the majority of development resources and have not always found it natural to coordinate.[8] It has also resulted in an increase in interagency transparency on the array of U.S. trade, development, and finance programs in operation in the four countries.

PfG has demonstrated that better strategic coordination can be achieved to some extent across agencies on priorities, and that a shared blueprint can achieve program-

4. "Fact Sheet: U.S. Global Development Policy," The White House, September 22, 2010, http://www.whitehouse.gov/the-press-office/2010/09/22/fact-sheet-us-global-development-policy.

5. Feed the Future is the administration's global hunger and food security initiative launched to implement a 2009 G-8 pledge at L'Aquila, Italy, to work with partner countries, development partners, and stakeholders, such as the private sector, to commit $3.5 billion to spur economic growth in agriculture. Grow Africa is an initiative launched by the African Union Commission, the Comprehensive Africa Agricultural Development Programme (CAADP), the New Partnership for Africa's Development (NEPAD) Agency, and the World Economic Forum in 2003 to accelerate private-sector investment in sustainable growth in African agriculture. In July 2013, President Obama launched Power Africa, a transaction-based approach to increase access to reliable, clean power in six countries (Ghana, Tanzania, Ethiopia, Nigeria, Kenya, and Liberia). All three initiatives are led by USAID within the U.S. government.

6. The methodology of the paper was based on off-the-record conversations with experts in the government, policy, nongovernmental, and academic communities, including senior officials involved in implementing Partnership for Growth in key agencies at various stages (USAID, MCC, Overseas Private Investment Corporation (OPIC), U.S. Trade and Development Agency (USTDA), NSC, U.S. Department of Commerce) and interested corporate partners regarding what donor tools are needed to mitigate risk enough to attract their capital to investments related to PfG priorities. Some PfG country implementers were also interviewed.

7. The Millennium Challenge Corporation (MCC) is a U.S. foreign assistance agency that has committed over $7.5 billion in five-year compacts and threshold programs for 36 developing countries. The program is distinguished by its competitive selection based on policy performance, its focus on country-led solutions and implementation, and its requirement for monitored, transparent results.

8. Although the USAID and MCC models are inherently complementary, with MCC focusing on long-term infrastructure programs and USAID focusing on annual, "softer" capacity-related projects.

matic synergies across U.S. development agencies. Coordination was less successful when strategic priorities of agencies did not intersect and is still limited across U.S. trade and development agencies.[9] This leaves unanswered, for further review, the broader, longstanding question of how to integrate U.S. trade and development programs so they are mutually reinforcing.

PfG also demonstrated that White House involvement can only go so far in achieving a coordinated trade and development strategy without programmatic budget alignment, and cannot overcome the varied mandates and jurisdictions of agencies. It can encourage, but cannot unilaterally accomplish, the U.S. Global Development Strategy's goal of a coordinated sustainable development strategy that engages non-aid actors.

In two PfG countries—El Salvador and Ghana—the MCC pursued more robust private-sector engagement that has provided a foundation for the co-design of projects with potential investors, and has helped target development resources on projects that will unlock the constraints of greatest interest to those investors.[10] These achievements would have occurred regardless of the PfG rubric and NSC involvement, but they represent a level of strategic coordination and learning across agencies, which is new and welcome territory for the U.S. government.

This paper argues that PfG began the paradigm shift toward a more coordinated and sustainable development strategy by highlighting the benefits of strategic coordination across agencies at the front end of an initiative. It also brought to light the difficulty of using development resources and tools to attract non-aid actors with what is still basically a government-to-government approach to development.

In that sense, PfG is making a significant contribution to a potential agenda for this and future administrations and presents a critical opportunity, regardless of the future of PfG itself. With three of the four PfG countries still in early stages of implementation, and with other experiments underway that can continue the momentum toward a more sustainable development model that integrates core business into development, there is still room to address the gaps and impediments in current strategy that limit our ability to fully harness the development impact of the private sector.

The challenges of taking PfG to the next level are possible to remedy in various degrees. These challenges include the inability to use authority to strategically align agency program budgets by the National Security Staff (NSS)[11] or Office of Management and Budget (OMB); the inability of a resource-constrained NSS to coordinate multiple agency strategies and budgets around a set of trade and development priorities; and missing incentives within the agencies to combine programs across agencies to greater effect and to engage non-aid actors. Some of these challenges require considerable reorientation, new resources, and in some cases, the consent of Congress.

Other challenges reflect the endemic structural limitations of U.S. trade and development architecture, such as different trade and development agency mandates and jurisdictions and policy restrictions that are vestiges of an era when the private sector was considered best left at arm's length in U.S. development strategy. Some would require organizational restructuring to address them fully, both within and among U.S. government agencies.[12]

The constituency in favor of making these changes exists but is diffuse, and without a strong advocacy effort to date, there is little consistent and constructive support to

---

9. For purposes of this paper, U.S. trade and development agencies include USAID, MCC, Overseas Private Investment Corporation (OPIC), U.S. Trade Representative (USTR), U.S. Trade Development Agency (USTDA), ExIm Bank (ExIm), U.S. Department of Commerce (USDOC), especially the U.S. Commercial Service (USCS), U.S. Department of the Treasury (Treasury), and can, depending on the initiative, include U.S. Department of Energy (USDOE) and the Foreign Agriculture Service (FAS) of the U.S. Department of Agriculture (USDA).

10. For example, General Electric, in close consultation with MCC and other donors, has signed a memorandum of understanding with the government of Ghana to build a 1,000-megawatt power plant over the next five years that will include a power park to strengthen the regulatory environment to attract other Independent Power Producers and provide management training for local operators.

11. In 2009, the National Security Council and Homeland Security Council were combined and are now referred to as the National Security Staff.

12. The Center for Global Development's Todd Moss argued for the worthy goal of streamlining development agency architecture, housing all U.S. government development finance tools in a new Development Bank. See Todd Moss, "Updating U.S. Foreign Assistance Tools and Development Policy for the Post-Aid World," testimony before the Senate Committee on Foreign Relations, Subcommittee on International Development and Foreign Operations, May 22, 2013, http://www.cgdev.org/sites/default/files/Moss%205%2022%2013%20SFRC%20Testimony_0.pdf.

encourage them within the administration or to help provide clear signals from Congress that they should be pursued.[13]

The U.S. government role in this new paradigm is facilitative, but could be far more transformative. If U.S. government priorities are clear—and PfG has demonstrated it is possible for U.S. development agencies to be on the same strategic page—and if resources are focused where they will have the most sustainable outcomes, with relevant processes and flexible tools, U.S. agencies can maximize opportunities for government agencies and non-aid actors to combine resources to greater developmental effect.

Elements of a sustainable development paradigm include:

- Leveraging core business and attracting foreign direct investment—Using development resources and tools to attract capital to development priorities and enhancing the developmental impact of ongoing or potential foreign direct investment is the most direct route to the higher incomes and skill levels, new jobs, and businesses that stimulate economic growth. Partnerships are one means to leverage and attract investment, and can result in positive outcomes. They should not, however, be confused as ends in themselves, or with the ultimate goal of attracting sustainable growth.

- Proactive approaches and a systemic process for investors to provide feedback and input in the initial stages of a development initiative in Washington and in country on how U.S. resources can be focused on the most sustainable projects in which the private sector is most likely to participate.

  Multi-stakeholder models that focus on the greatest impediments to planned or potential investments in the enabling environment, by encouraging a three-way conversation with the host government, U.S. development agencies, and the private sector—in particular,

foreign and local investors.[14] These conversations can help specifically identify the "but/for," that is, what specifically is keeping a particular company from investing? The development agency can then focus its resources and tools accordingly to address the gaps identified by the private sector, and focus its negotiations with the beneficiary government on the regulatory changes needed for the project to succeed.

New capabilities and incentives within U.S. government agencies for staff to understand and leverage the long-term strategies and goals of companies interested in investing and sourcing with developmental impact, and incentives to use U.S. government resources and tools to attract investment, and enhance the developmental impact of a company's planned investments. Ensuring that missions and Millennium Challenge accountable entities in country have the expectation, incentives, and capability, in terms of both resources and staff, to use development resources to attract investment.

New tools flexibly applied to specific transactions that mitigate the higher risk, cost, and longer time horizons required to achieve sustainable commercial viability of most investment in high-growth, high-need markets. This can include, for example, government activities that combine efforts on pre-feasibility work and due diligence for investors; providing the capacity to speed evaluation of environmental and land use permits, use of grants for funds, sunset support, partial risk, credit and capital guarantees; creative capacity building that provides transactional, regulatory, and advisory support to help governments negotiate Power Purchase Agreements (PPAs) and concession agreements; and advice on structuring Public-Private Partnerships (PPPs). ▶

---

13. See, for example, H.R. 6178, sponsored by Representative Steve Chabot (R-OH) to establish an interagency mechanism to coordinate U.S. development programs and private-sector investment activities. Senator Johnny Isaakson (R-GA) has companion legislation in the Senate. Both call for many elements of PfG, such as coordination and engagement of the private sector in the early stages of project development, in Washington and in country. Representative Ed Royce (R-CA) is also considering the Electrify Africa Act of 2013 (the introduced version of the bill appears here: http://www.govtrack.us/congress/bills/113/hr2548/text). The bill asks the administration to develop a multiyear strategy to help sub-Saharan African countries access electricity by facilitating power projects through expedited loan guarantees, grants, insurance, and other U.S. government tools.
14. Grow Africa and Power Africa have adopted multi-stakeholder approaches.

CHAPTER 1
Introduction

Aid alone is not development. Development is helping nations actually develop…moving from poverty to prosperity. And we need more than just aid to unleash that change. We need to harness all the tools at our disposal. —*President Barack Obama*

The administration's Presidential Policy Directive (PPD) of September 2010 set goals for a new U.S. Development Policy. Among other things, it called for an increased programmatic focus on "sustainable development outcomes" that place a premium on broad-based economic growth and "game-changing innovations."

The directive announced a "reorientation" of approach to make economic growth a cornerstone of U.S. development strategy. It also articulated the goal of providing a more integral role for the private sector—from "policy conception to implementation," to more readily leverage the resources of other actors, and to bring to bear all of the tools of the U.S. government toward common development objectives.

More recent reports reflecting the views of key stakeholders in U.S. development strategy have reinforced this conclusion, and reiterated the need to reorient U.S. development strategy around private-sector-led growth.[15]

New operational models are fundamental to achieve this vision—models that catch up to the revolution underway in how resources are allocated to solve development problems. There is an imperative to go beyond the traditional paradigm where donor funding is the predominant development resource, "development" is largely a conversation between governments and donors, and companies essentially "write a check" for development projects in the hope that sustainable outcomes will follow. Donors invest in projects assuming "if we build it, the private sector will come." Corporations dedicate resources to projects that often fall under the umbrella of "corporate social responsibility." Both may have an impact but often are implemented in parallel (or even at cross

---

15. The CSIS Executive Council on Development concluded that the United States could increase the impact of U.S. development assistance by making broad-based growth the central organizing principle of U.S. development policy, aligning U.S. development instruments with the private sector, and promoting trade and investment using existing but underutilized tools. See CSIS Executive Council on Development, *Our Shared Opportunity: A Vision for Global Prosperity* (Washington, DC: CSIS, March 2013), http://csis.org/files/publication/130304_Nesseth_DevCouncilReport_Web.pdf.

purposes) but miss the opportunity to capture the transformation that is more likely to occur when donors and the private sector leverage each other's core competencies.

While there is clearer understanding of the more robust outcomes that come from raising incomes, lifting skill levels, and creating new businesses that only the private sector can provide, the existing development agency architecture is still evolving to strategically engage non-aid actors. The need for U.S. development agencies to streamline the architecture around engaging the private sector has been discussed in a number of analyses.[16]

Partnership for Growth (PfG)—along with Feed the Future (FtF)—were the administration's initial experiments to apply a new model of development to four countries in the case of PfG, and to 19 countries in the case of FtF. PfG's signature goals were to increase coherence across agencies and bring to bear non-aid resources to unlock new sources of foreign direct investment. More effective outcomes would be the result, by going beyond traditional trade and development models to fully engage more partners, particularly the private sector, and to leverage public and private resources through greater government coordination.[17]

This paper is about what the PfG experiment has taught us about how to move toward a sustainable development model—as Partnership for Growth, Feed the Future, Power Africa, Millennium Challenge Corporation (MCC), or any other development initiative.

It draws conclusions about achievements, lessons learned, and strategic gaps and proposes new U.S. government approaches that the private sector could find useful to align its investment strategies with U.S. development priorities. It attempts to demystify the "how" of engaging the core business of companies in a new model of private-sector-led development, from a donor's perspective.[18] And it argues that a direct approach, achievable during the Obama administration and requiring few, if any, new resources could be for development agencies to focus on improving and coordinating the process, incentives and tools around specific projects, while the debate continues around the architecture of U.S. trade and development programs. ▶

---

16. The CSIS Executive Council on Development report (*Our Shared Opportunity*), cited above, points out that while the United States has some of the best development agencies in the world, they were designed at a time when U.S. capital flows were primarily public. Indeed, public flows are now less than 10 percent of the equation (p. 5). The Executive Council grappled with how U.S. government agency tools can be used more creatively and flexibly to leverage the developmental impact of private investment (pp. 23–29).
17. U.S. Department of State, "Partnership for Growth," fact sheet, November 29, 2011, http://www.state.gov/r/pa/prs/ps/2011/11/177887.htm.
18. The focus of this paper is on elements of a sustainable development model, not on all elements of what PfG set out to achieve. Other innovations called for by the PPD, such as greater focus on country ownership, selectivity, and impact evaluation, are not discussed.

CHAPTER 2
What Has Partnership for Growth Taught Us about Sustainable Development?

What were the most important takeaways from the PfG experiment?

▶ National Security Staff (NSS) involvement brings greater coordination and transparency of agency programs, but deeper coherence across agency programs requires greater NSS authority and capacity.

What has made the Partnership for Growth process[19] unique, compared to the development of MCC compacts, Feed the Future, Power Africa, or any other economic development priority, is greater NSS engagement. This has included hands-on management of a dedicated interagency process that strongly encouraged—but has not forced—all trade and development agencies to align relevant programs to a PfG Joint Country Action Plan[20] or, when being negotiated simultaneously, an MCC compact, as in the case of El Salvador and Ghana.

The NSS is involved in several trade and development processes, but few are chaired and managed by the NSS. PfG is unique in the degree of NSS interest in a coordinated strategy, in part because PfG was conceived to operationalize the PPD that called for a more inclusive, coherent development strategy.

Indeed, greater NSS involvement is one possible solution often offered to address the relative disconnection between U.S. trade and development programs.[21]

One of the lessons PfG can teach, then, is whether a stronger NSS role—and the necessary capacity and competencies needed to go with it[22]—on trade and development priorities is a viable solution to this longstanding problem.

---

19. The selection process for choosing PfG countries is not public, but interviews suggest that meeting MCC criteria (such as the control of corruption and democracy indicators) and performing well in implementing MCC compacts were key selection factors, indicators that U.S. development resources have been relatively well spent.

20. A Joint Country Action Plan was negotiated between U.S. lead agencies and reflected areas of focus that generally tracked an economic "constraints analysis" jointly undertaken by MCC, USAID, and State Department country economists. For example, in El Salvador, Joint Country Action Plans focused on security and trade infrastructure. In Tanzania, the focus was access to finance and power generation.

21. A CSIS report noted that "The United States can and should do more with its trade and development agendas to ensure they achieve mutually supportive goals. But as of now, the U.S. government has no specific strategy to do so outside the negotiation of trade agreements, nor any office empowered with the necessary resources to implement such a strategy." See CSIS Executive Council on Development, *Our Shared Opportunity: A Vision for Global Prosperity* (Washington, DC: CSIS, March 2013), p. 27, http://csis.org/files/publication/130304_Nesseth_DevCouncilReport_Web.pdf.

22. The ability of the NSS to sustainably manage and coordinate any issue is naturally limited by the ebb and flow of key personnel, their interests, and the array of priorities before them.

Many interviewed participating in the PfG process observed achievements in terms of transparency of the number and variations of agency programs that could be brought to bear on specific PfG priorities.

However, as it is, the NSS could only go so far when it came to actually aligning programs, budgets, and strategic priorities across agencies. Better alignment occurred across the development agencies that share similar budgetary authority and congressional jurisdictions, but strategic alignment between the development and trade agencies was still illusive. Trade agencies did not participate in the constraints analyses, and therefore had little buy-in in the formation of a PfG country's strategic roadmap. Some suggested the current process could not support existing Joint Country Action Plan implementation and could certainly become unsustainable if additional countries were added to the process, with no new dedicated resources.

Greater coherence would require taking NSS involvement to the next level, including deeper involvement in the budget process to force alignment and identify and create synergies across programs. To date, this has proven to be a bridge too far and unmanageable for NSS's limited capacity and what was already by many accounts a cumbersome process.

It would also require dedicated resources for the initiative, to create the incentive for agencies to participate without the undesirable truth of an unfunded mandate.[23]

Without dedicated resources, there has been a noted disincentive for coordination, as agencies resist putting their programs on the table, lest the programs become vulnerable to possible funding cuts. This problem is exacerbated and complicated by the absence of alignment in congressional jurisdictions or across appropriation bills.

Similarly, without resources to co-invest with other actors, and limited capacity to use programs to attract private funding, private actors have little incentive to engage. It may

not be a coincidence that the most effective private-sector outreach and input was directly related to the development of MCC compacts, where the private sector saw available resources with which to collaborate.

White House oversight is insufficient to leverage the resources of non-aid actors, especially without resources to leverage.

In the case of PfG, NSS involvement has been useful in providing needed strategic coordination at the front end of establishing a development priority, and in providing transparency to encourage agencies to share strategic priorities when they intersect. NSS oversight has brought coordination that would not otherwise have occurred and had rarely occurred before across agencies—particularly in terms of shared constraints analyses, greater program coordination of some agencies (e.g., USAID around MCC compacts), and greater programmatic transparency.

When trade and development agency strategic priorities do not intersect, the NSS did not have the capacity to align programs. This is not only a question of NSS capacity and ability to use Office of Management and Budget (OMB) authority to align programs that cut across various budget accounts in four countries, but the fact that U.S. agencies have different mandates, business models, and congressional jurisdictions.[24] This problem could become more acute as PfG Joint Country Action Plans are implemented.

PfG has shown us, then, that NSS involvement in a priority initiative can achieve a significant degree of strategic coordination across trade and development programs. This coordination is fundamental to engaging non-aid actors, but it is not sufficient. Relying on greater NSS involvement alone to achieve more sustainable development is not a long-term strategy. As implementation demands of PfG intensify, or if new countries are added to the initiative, NSS management of PfG could become increasingly unsustainable.[25]

---

23. However, at a time when other agency program funding has been falling, USAID has been able to maintain its funding for the four PfG countries.
24. The State Department, USAID, MCC, Overseas Private Investment Corporation (OPIC), Ex-Im Bank, and U.S. Trade Development Agency (USTDA) submit their budget proposals under the international affairs account ("150 account"), while the trade agencies largely submit their budgets to the account that manages Commerce, Justice, Science, and other related agencies.
25. Some suggested a solution could be for one agency to be given the lead for PfG. Similarly, USAID was given the lead on Feed the Future after what some considered a confusing start, and most argued that the program benefited from this clarity in its ability to coordinate other agencies around the program. However, if one agency were given the lead on PfG, budget authority would have to accompany it to enable that agency to coordinate resources from other agencies. In the case of Feed the Future, although USAID controls about 90 percent of program resources, budget battles continue among agencies. PfG funding is largely scattered across agencies, which would further complicate a similar approach.

▶ Coordination increases when a strategic blueprint is shared across agencies.

A significant benefit of the PfG experiment was the shared development of an economic constraints analysis between USAID, MCC, and the Department of State, and the use of the analysis as a strategic "roadmap" for PfG discussions around Joint Country Action Plans.

The concept behind using an analysis of the most binding constraints to economic growth[26] to determine how U.S. development resources are spent and how development projects are chosen was pioneered by MCC as a first step in developing MCC compacts. Its purpose is to focus U.S. development resources on projects that will have the greatest impact on economic growth in a country, based on a jointly undertaken economic analysis, which then serves as a basis for projects that will be designed and developed by the country.

Within a government-to-government model, constraints analyses have been useful in narrowing the conversation with country partners about which sectors of the economy should be the focus of U.S. development resources. It provides a transparent, objective rationale for project definition that helps narrow projects from a long list of developmental, and often political, priorities.

Constraints analyses have been an important innovation for development by providing an economic foundation for a country-owned approach. PfG's innovation was to share the development of this analysis across several U.S. government agencies, which then served as a strategic blueprint for coordination across agencies (and between the U.S. and partner country governments) that had to date been missing in U.S. trade and development programs.[27] These analyses have generally pointed toward major infrastructure. Other constraints, such as transportation, access to finance, limited trade capacity, agriculture productivity, and access to reliable power also have been highlighted.

Another benefit of the PfG process was greater coordination of government programs around MCC compacts, which, when developed in synch with PfG Joint Country Action Plans, at least aligned the MCC compact with USAID programs. This is a significant occurrence, because MCC compacts have been largely negotiated between the beneficiary government and MCC, without the benefit of strategic coordination with other U.S. trade and development agencies. While there has been some coordination with USAID, program coordination with other U.S. government programs has been difficult to achieve.

The PfG process also brought to light that agency alignment is most successful when PfG designation is synched at the start of MCC compact development and based on the same constraints analysis. If Joint Country Action Plans are negotiated out of synch with an MCC five-year compact, coordination is marginal at best. For example, El Salvador's Joint Country Action Plan had little in common with El Salvador's first MCC compact. However El Salvador's second compact and constraints analysis were synched with the PfG Joint Country Action Plan, allowing for coordination.

This suggests the next wave of PfG countries should prioritize MCC countries where a new compact is just underway to maximize outcomes.[28]

---

26. An economic constraints analysis is a diagnostic of what the major macroeconomic constraints to growth are in an economy. See Ricardo Hausmann, Dani Rodrik, and AndrésVelasco, "Growth Diagnostics," in *The Washington Consensus Reconsidered: Towards a New Global Governance*, ed. Narcís Serra and Joseph E. Stiglitz (New York: Oxford University Press, 2008).

27. Some noted the growing voices, including among ambassadors and mission directors, calling for a constraints-to-growth process in all aid-recipient countries, not just for MCC and PfG.

28. An interagency decision has been made to add one or two countries to the initiative, but to postpone deciding which countries to include. Were the administration to make the next wave of countries eligible for MCC compact PfG countries, at this writing, those countries include Liberia, Sierra Leon, Niger, and Morocco. Tanzania is now negotiating a second MCC compact, but is already a PfG country.

Perhaps because most PfG Joint Country Action Plans are still new to U.S. development strategy, the experiment has not yet translated into a blueprint for strategic priorities in country. Those interviewed thought there was still some distance to go in achieving coordination across agencies of complementary programs at the mission level.

That said, PfG did provide a rationale for initiatives that could combine trade and development tools. For example:

- In El Salvador, a Growth Council was created to improve dialogue between the public and private sector—both of which had longstanding suspicion of each other—on how development resources could be focused to increase investment.

- An education initiative was launched to help El Salvadoran vocational institutions provide training relevant to the private sector and potential investors.

- In the Philippines, the country furthest along in the PfG process, more than $160 million of the economic growth budget was recast from underutilized basic education programs in Mindanao for tertiary and vocational educational programs in high demand by the private sector.

But these were exceptions to the general observation that a country's strategic plan did not reflect PfG priorities, and strategic plans in PfG countries that coordinated programs across agencies and with the private sector were missing. Companies still perceive a disconnect between the rhetoric of both proposed legislation and agencies that call for greater leveraging of mission strategic plans with the private sector and the processes available to enable them to follow through.

▶ Government-to-government strategies are limited in their ability to attract non-aid actors.

U.S. development agencies are becoming increasingly aware that engaging the core business of companies is key to sustainable development, and that it must be harnessed for U.S. development programs to achieve broad-based economic growth.

Yet because agency architecture, processes, and tools to support a private-sector-led model are still evolving, agencies have met a challenge using development resources to attract foreign direct investment, beyond corporate philanthropy.

In a government-to-government model, there are few incentives—within the agencies or within partner government ministries—to go through the labor-intensive and bureaucratically different process of identifying the intersection, where partners have overlapping core business goals and how to leverage their resources. Developing and implementing projects are difficult enough, without the added burden of finding the right partner(s) and aligning efforts.

In a private-sector-led approach, this problem can be overcome with more appropriate incentives within the agencies and with a process focused on attracting potential partners with overlapping interests.

Current processes grounded in a government-to-government model are based on assumptions that the only appropriate public-sector role for development agencies is to fund public goods. With some exceptions, processes and tools that can help change the risk equation for an investor and thereby attract investment to development priorities are in an early stage of development at USAID and MCC.

Government-to-government processes also generally do not lead to solutions that result in development resources provided directly to private actors, although agencies have the statutory authority to do so.[29] This is the case even if those resources catalyze private-sector investment that will raise income levels, stimulate new businesses, and potentially generate new U.S. exports or otherwise meet U.S. trade and development goals.[30]

These are structural limitations within a government-to-government model that limit the ability to engage non-aid actors and core business.

29. Congress provided MCC with the statutory mandate to provide grants to private actors (Public Law 108-199, Title VI, Millennium Challenge Corporation Act of 2003, http://www.mcc.gov/documents/reports/mca_legislation.pdf). USAID also provides grants to private actors, primarily through technical assistance. In a January 25, 2010, letter from then-Senators John Kerry (D-MA) and Richard Lugar (R-IN) to MCC CEO Daniel Yohannes, the senators also clarified that MCC should seek full private-sector participation in the conceptualization and implementation of projects.
30. There are legitimate concerns about providing grants without appropriate safeguards to "favorite" private-sector actors, or providing subsidies to companies that ultimately fail, which can discourage agencies from pushing the envelope on innovative uses of government resources.

Partnership for Growth Initiative

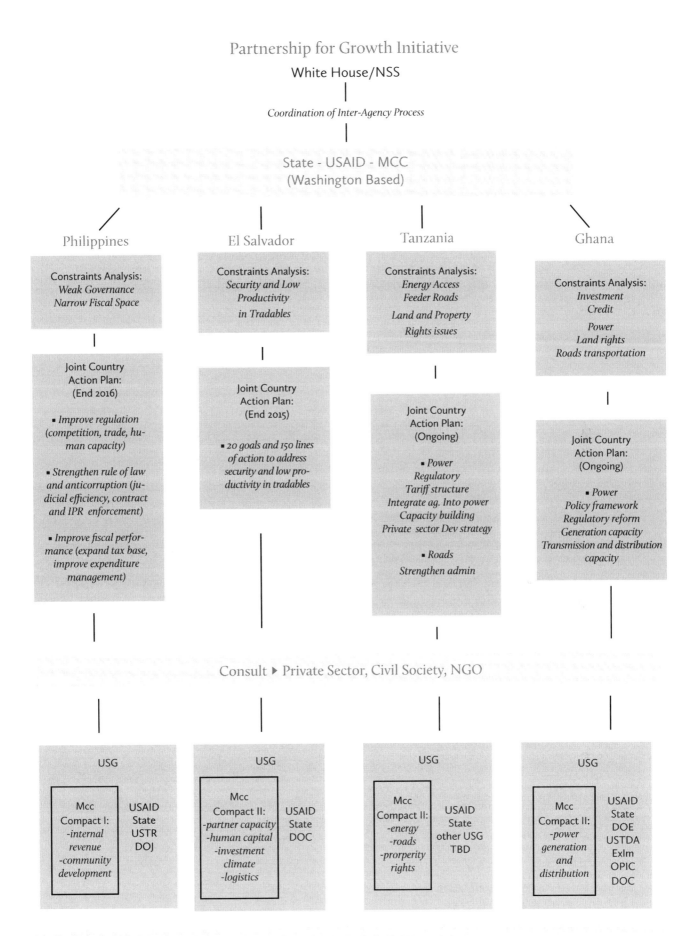

White House/NSS

Coordination of Inter-Agency Process

State - USAID - MCC
(Washington Based)

Philippines

Constraints Analysis:
*Weak Governance
Narrow Fiscal Space*

Joint Country
Action Plan:
(End 2016)

• *Improve regulation
(competition, trade, human capacity)*

• *Strengthen rule of law
and anticorruption (judicial efficiency, contract
and IPR enforcement)*

• *Improve fiscal performance (expand tax base,
improve expenditure
management)*

El Salvador

Constraints Analysis:
*Security and Low
Productivity
in Tradables*

Joint Country
Action Plan:
(End 2015)

• *20 goals and 150 lines
of action to address
security and low productivity in tradables*

Tanzania

Constraints Analysis:
*Energy Access
Feeder Roads

Land and Property

Rights issues*

Joint Country
Action Plan:
(Ongoing)

• *Power
Regulatory
Tariff structure
Integrate ag. Into power
Capacity building
Private sector Dev strategy*

• *Roads
Strengthen admin*

Ghana

Constraints Analysis:
*Investment
Credit

Power
Land rights
Roads transportation*

Joint Country
Action Plan:
(Ongoing)

• *Power
Policy framework
Regulatory reform
Generation capacity
Transmission and distribution
capacity*

Consult ▶ Private Sector, Civil Society, NGO

USG	USG	USG	USG
Mcc Compact I: -*internal revenue* -*community development* / USAID State USTR DOJ	Mcc Compact II: -*partner capacity* -*human capital* -*investment climate* -*logistics* / USAID State DOC	Mcc Compact II: -*energy* -*roads* -*prorperty rights* / USAID State other USG TBD	Mcc Compact II: -*power generation and distribution* / USAID State DOE USTDA ExIm OPIC DOC

Monitoring and Evaluation

Consequently, it is often difficult for a potential investor that could make a project sustainable to find the opportunities and the tools to make the difference—provide "the tipping point," to lower the risks of an investment enough to justify it in the near term.

One goal of PfG was to leverage the resources of non-aid actors. However, because PfG has no independent funding, is focused on addressing macroeconomic constraints, rather than removing the constraints of specific projects, and is still largely a conversation between governments, the PfG framework is grounded in a "build it and they will come" model. Its primary goal is to serve as a vehicle for governments to jointly address the most binding constraints to growth, based on a data-driven analysis with limited input from current or prospective investors. This approach assumes that once governments have set the table, so to speak, investors will come and dine.

Indeed, most U.S. development has been largely based on this approach, whether Joint Country Action Plans, MCC compacts, or Feed the Future. It is difficult to align development and company strategies when investors are not involved in the discussion regarding which development projects to choose.

The only option for the private sector to participate, under this scenario, is to be grafted into project choices already agreed to by governments. Any alignment with a company's investment strategy and core business is coincidence at best.

Tapping the sustainable solutions only the private sector can bring to development projects—added resources, scope, reach, capacity, training, supply chain development, and the new jobs, skills, and businesses that go with it—is much more likely when the project is designed or at least consistent with a company's business strategy from the beginning. Investors are more likely to come to the table when they know what's for dinner.

A dynamic can also be created that attracts new companies and inspires new investment in alignment with development priorities, particularly if they are now aware of the opportunity to leverage and see available tools to mitigate risk, address capacity needs, or otherwise speed the timetable of commercial viability. For example, Coca-Cola would not have gone forward with a project sourcing fruit from smallholder farmers, but was able to proceed on a commercially sustainable basis with donor and nonprofit support, given the clear training and income benefits for targeted farmers.[31] A company would be willing to source from a Feed the Future supply chain, but to reach commercial viability doing so would need targeted capacity building that helps farmers reach volume and quality standards for market.

The argument here is not that companies determine U.S. development priorities, but that once the basic framework of an initiative is agreed, such as a sector or country focus, and shared across agencies, the investors that development agencies want to attract are part of an early conversation to help determine how to make the investment commercially possible and developmentally impactful.

Notably, in the case of El Salvador and Ghana,[32] MCC had multiple detailed conversations early in the development of their second compacts—both in country and in Washington. These conversations went beyond pro forma consultations with local chambers of commerce, and included proactive outreach to more than 200 domestic and international companies. In particular, it led to a commitment from a major energy producer to make a significant investment related to Ghana's second MCC compact.[33] The process helped focus resources on the constraints of greatest interest to real-time investors, and will help inform the design of projects that could address key gaps in the investment environment. USAID had conversations with investors early in the PfG process to obtain feedback on the investment environment in all four countries as well.

---

31. See TechnoServe, "Nurturing New Opportunities for Fruit Famers in East Africa," http://www.technoserve.org/our-work/stories/nurturing-new-opportunities-for-fruit-farmers-in-east-africa.
32. MCC intends to pursue this "Investment Opportunity Assessment" approach in the case of Tanzania as well. Previously, MCC projects were based solely on the results of constraints analyses, without the benefit of company feedback on what limited investment.
33. See Anthony Sedzro, "General Electric to Build 1000MW Power Plant in Ghana," *Ventures*, June 30, 2013, http://www.ventures-africa.com/2013/06/general-electric-to-build-1000mw-power-plant-in-ghana/.

MCC would have undertaken this more robust approach with the private sector regardless of the PfG process. However the engagement can inform other frameworks regarding how to move beyond government-led approaches.[34]

Government to Government Model: Private Sector Participation

PFG - MCC - FTF

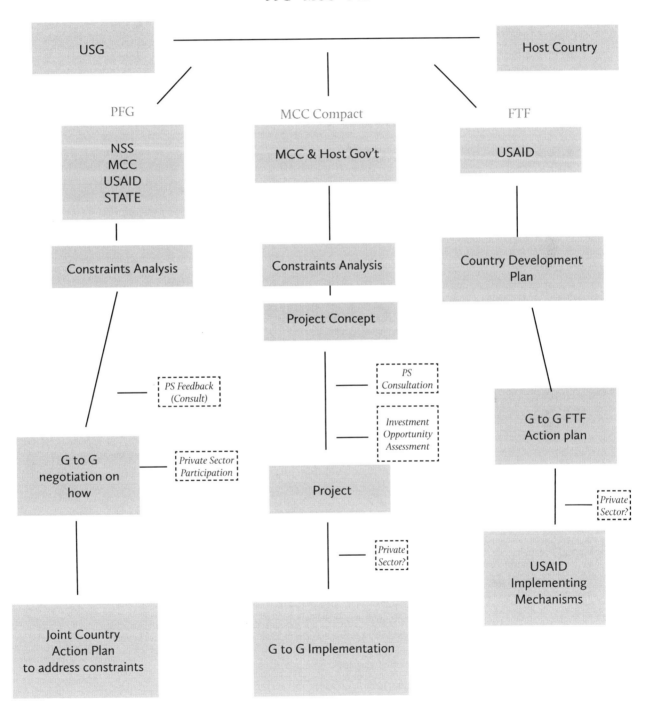

34. And some of the initiative's best lessons—such as the advantage of sharing a blueprint across agencies to focus programs—are being replicated in non-PfG countries, such as Tunisia and Morocco. Interestingly, that exercise brought to light the fact that current U.S. government spending is not aligned with the most binding constraints to economic growth.

CHAPTER 3
Toward Sustainable Development: Process, Incentives, and Tools

What, then, is the most effective way for the U.S. government to achieve sustainable development? How can agencies go beyond theoretical calls for greater participation of the private sector in development, and apply it on the ground?

Practically speaking, a new paradigm would recognize and embrace the shared interest of government and investors in lowering the risk of sustainable investment. It would look at new ways to use existing resources more flexibly to enable companies to reevaluate the risk profile of a particular investment in high-risk, but developmentally impactful sectors, by raising its investment premium and lowering the risk.

When companies decide whether to make an investment in a country where the commercial, legal, regulatory, or policy framework is weak, or the political or economic environment is potentially unstable, their discount rate and the reasonable rate of return required to justify the investment is relatively high compared to other investments, particularly if it is in new, unfamiliar territory for a company.

This fact of life is part of the fabric of some U.S. development agencies. The Overseas Private Investment Corporation (OPIC), for example, provides long-term debt, political risk insurance, convertibility insurance, and other tools to lower the risk of investment in developing countries. The Development Credit Authority at USAID provides partial loan guarantees to local private finance institutions to lower their perceived risk of financing underserved borrowers.

But most U.S. development program funding was not originally designed to be leveraged, utilized to mitigate risk, or systematically attract sustainable investment.[35] U.S. government tools are still catching up to achieve this goal. Yet investment and the economic growth it brings will not occur unless costs and risks can be lowered enough for a company to make a reasonable rate of return.

This is the missing catalyst in a government-to-government model.

SUSTAINABLE DEVELOPMENT PROCESS

A sustainable development process begins where development priorities and the interests of investors intersect, and focuses on what investors need to invest in those priorities. It recognizes that sustainable outcomes are difficult to achieve without identifying where development priorities and investment strategies overlap, and that gaining traction in leveraging resources where develop-

---

35. Additionally, much of USAID's development resources are earmarked for health, education, and other service delivery; economic growth funding overall is often most vulnerable to budget cuts, even when the administration prioritizes it.

ment goals and investment strategies intersect requires more aggressive risk mitigation.

It is distinct from most U.S. development agency processes in that it actively courts private capital using development finance tools and resources.

The starting point is either existing projects, or the proactive identification of potential investors that are interested in investing in or around a development priority. Country and sector investment priorities are determined by the initiatives (e.g., Power Africa, Grow Africa, Feed the Future) or through a constraints analysis that could focus on the question of where investment will be both viable and have the most catalytic impact on poverty. Projects that result are generally in sectors or supply chains that disrupt poverty, but require greater risk mitigation to reach commercial viability.

Projects are the fulcrum for the coordination of interagency support, possibly with one agency designated lead and empowered by the NSS to coordinate a package of appropriate capacity-building and development finance tools across the government to bring the project forward. An OPIC loan could be combined with USAID or U.S. Trade and Development Agency (USTDA) capacity building or feasibility support, or a Development Credit Authority (DCA) or MCC grant could be brought to bear as needed as guarantees to address gaps jointly identified by investors and governments.

The goal of the process would be to bring a project to financial closure, help mitigate risk throughout implementation, and expand the project's developmental reach, affordability, and impact. In the case of new projects, once potential investors are identified, the U.S. government facilitates a trilateral process to identify gaps that governments can fill. In the case of initiatives that are not focused on constraints, rather than projects (the case with PfG), companies can help identify which collaborative efforts would most likely help attract their investment in the future.

What is different in this approach is that the coordination process revolves around the investment, and government efforts are focused on supporting and filling identified gaps in the project and ways to enhance its developmental impact. It is distinct from a process where private actors try to graft their engagement into broader development goals.

Under that scenario, because it is so much more difficult to find the intersection between a development priority and core business, resulting partnerships generally involve company corporate social responsibility activities, rather than co-investment.

Using the investment or the attraction of the investment as the focal point is a more direct route to leverage non-aid actors, and has the greatest potential to focus development resources where they will be most sustainable, with the demand side of the equation factored in to project choice, design, and development. A project focused on increasing agricultural productivity, for example, could be designed in consultation with potential buyers who can provide buyer guarantees and inform post-harvest infrastructure.

Private-sector participation in project scoping also helps allay one of the biggest obstacles to leveraging U.S. government resources, which is the inability to synch company investment strategies with USAID and MCC project funding cycles.[36]

Both U.S. and host governments are highly involved in the process, but as conveners and catalysts. They contribute *at the margin* to provide the necessary capacity building, risk mitigation, and advocacy to remove policy and regulatory barriers directly related to projects to accelerate project development and create a dynamic that attracts new investors and stakeholders to participate in development solutions.

The resulting multi-stakeholder conversation involving the U.S. and partner governments around the necessary policy, legal and regulatory changes to support specific transactions can create a more powerful incentive for host governments to make what are often politically challenging changes when real-time investors are at the table, and can be more powerful than broad-based advocacy or conditional assistance.

---

36. For example, significant consultations with the private sector around the development of Ghana's second compact will help address potential investor capacity-building needs. Ghana's first compact, in contrast, had already spent resources on supporting infrastructure less relevant to private-sector needs when a private partner appeared. Because the compact was well into implementation, the only option to satisfy company and market requirements was to retrofit the compact or increase the debt of compact beneficiaries.

Proposed Sustainable Development Model
Private Sector Participation

Power Africa, Grow Africa

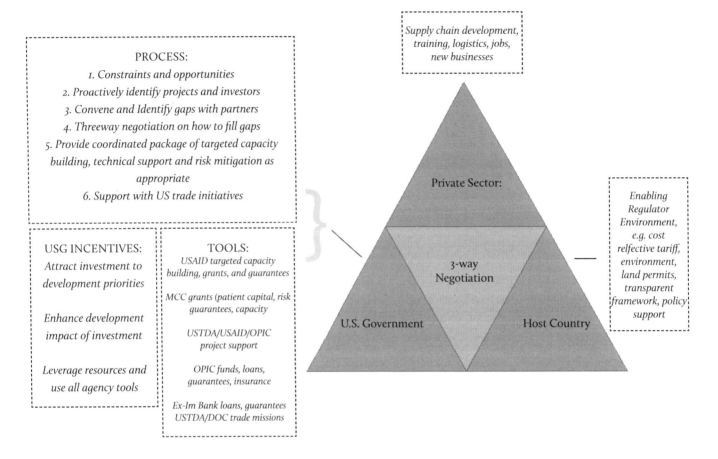

SUSTAINABLE DEVELOPMENT INCENTIVES

Key to a more sustainable development model is agency incentives—in Washington and at missions—for staff to be aware of and be rewarded for leveraging corporate investment strategies with government resources for development goals.

Agencies are moving in this direction. USAID missions must leverage 1 percent of their budgets with Global Development Alliance and Development Credit Authority programs. Field Investment Officers, who are trained and rewarded on the basis of transactions with the local and international private sector, have been deployed to seven countries.[37] New "Relationship Managers" are now established to enable longer-term strategic relationships between companies and USAID that can cut across multiple country missions, and provide capacity to leverage company strategies. They can also provide headquarter support to help facilitate mission partnerships and could serve as a vehicle for agency staff to gain a better understanding of corporate strategies.

---

37. Investment officers are now in Kenya, Nigeria, South Africa, Thailand, Egypt, Peru, and Ukraine.

These steps could be strengthened by:

- Setting as a performance goal—perhaps even providing monetary incentives for—the attraction of investment that meets development goals, and the use of U.S. development resources and tools to complement the developmental impact of company investments and sourcing patterns;

- Providing capacity for missions and MCC accountable entities to leverage resources with non-aid actors where possible, by:

  - ▶ Strengthening personnel in missions[38] and Millennium Challenge Account entities in countries to leverage private-sector actors[39];

  - ▶ Providing dedicated funding at missions and in compacts to respond to real-time project-related requests, where company and development goals intersect;

  - ▶ Supporting analytic capacity to identify potential investors;

  - ▶ Increasing budget targets of resources that could be leveraged with the private sector or non-aid actors in the case of missions, and establishing compact targets and expectations in the case of MCC compacts;

  - ▶ Empowering agencies in Washington and on the ground to use a range of U.S. development tools from a number of agencies to increase the developmental impact of their investments.[40]

Creating incentives to encourage agencies to use company sustainable activities as platforms for U.S. government capacity-building activities, rather than the reverse, is another effective private-sector-led approach. For example, some companies are investing significant resources in improving the livelihoods of the communities where they invest, including considerable resources dedicated to state and local institutional capacity building. Core business interests intersect with donor strategies, for example, when they invest in building new supply chains and other backward linkages in the domestic economy. These investments can be several times greater with much longer time horizons than most donor funding cycles. Targeting agency programs to enhance these private-sector efforts is a sustainable approach and would provide an incentive for more companies to take the lead in sponsoring sustainable investment.[41]

SUSTAINABLE DEVELOPMENT TOOLS

Creative Capacity Building

Because time is money, one of the most significant ways U.S. tools can stimulate investment is to accelerate the project development cycle by strengthening the capabilities of the host government and lowering pre-development costs. Capacity gaps in specific projects and value chains are often the greatest risk of an investment at the outset, and aggressive use of technical assistance by government agencies can tip the balance to earlier commercial viability.

---

38. For example, with U.S. Commercial Service personnel at USAID trade hubs, additional field investment officers, or by using foreign service nationals. A broader policy question is whether and how to strengthen the U.S. Department of Commerce's Commercial Service presence in developing countries.

39. MCC is now requiring accountable entities to hire local personnel dedicated to private-sector outreach. MCC has authority to use capacity-building resources under 609(g) of its authorizing statute to help a country develop a compact, which have been to date largely untapped to identify potential private-sector partners to invest with or around compact priorities.

40. This goes to the question of how to more effectively link U.S. trade and development initiatives so they are mutually reinforcing. Encouraging MCC compacts that support the U.S. trade agenda (e.g., providing capacity building to take advantage of U.S. free-trade agreements or preference programs, or focusing compacts on trade facilitation to encourage investment) or broadening incentives and capacity for U.S. Trade Representative, Commerce, and State to support U.S. development goals.

41. See Chevron Corporation's Niger Delta Partnership Initiative, http://ndpifoundation.org.

Companies cited the need for early-stage costs related to project development, which often present the greatest obstacle to an investment, and could be shared. Companies interested in investing in the energy sector in Africa, for example, indicated that it was the first $10 million in project development costs that presented the greatest hurdle, especially when a country's regulatory and legal structure was uncertain and capacity in partner governments and utilities was limited. USAID and MCC have started to look in this direction in the energy sector.[42]

Capacity building was the area where the intersection of interests was greatest between U.S. government agencies and companies. Enabling state and local governments to be efficient and predictable partners with the international and local private sector, and growing the institutional capacity to sustain that ability, was cited as an area where U.S. development agencies could have great impact. More targeted U.S. government support in these areas would both incentivize investment and expand a project's reach, scope, and affordability.

Although capacity building was one of the most catalytic ways the U.S. government could provide support, it was also the area noted to be the most uncoordinated, duplicative, and underutilized aspect of U.S. government programs.

Companies were generally unaware of the tools that agencies had available, or found them difficult to access and deploy for specific project needs to lower risk to an investor. Some indicated they would rather assume the greater cost of going it alone than spend the time and effort to understand how to leverage U.S. programs. Traditional, generic capacity building applied across the board to address broad-based country needs was not considered relevant to investor needs.

Lack of flexibility around USAID budgetary planning cycles and limited windows during which funding can be leveraged under MCC compacts were key constraints for agencies to be responsive to non-aid partners. Companies cannot anticipate their project needs at the exact time windows open on mission budget and MCC compact

three- and five-year planning cycles, and many companies find synching their investment strategies into those planning cycles problematic.

Companies[43] indicated strong interest in assuming or sharing costs on:

- Pre-feasibility work in high-need, high-risk countries can cost in the millions of dollars and take significantly more time than in traditional markets. This includes basic capacity of a country to negotiate PPPs; transactional, regulatory, and advisory support to help governments and utilities negotiate PPAs; off-take and concession agreements; and shared due diligence of the gaps in a country's regulatory regime. Policy support to establish a commercially viable tariff structure is key.

- Feasibility work, including shared or reimbursable funding for bankable studies. While U.S. Trade Development Agency (USTDA) feasibility studies were cited as helpful, in energy and infrastructure in particular, USTDA did not have the available resources to develop bankable studies on which a transaction could obtain funding.

- Post-feasibility work, including transaction advisors for requests for proposals (RFPs) and to structure Public-Private Partnerships (PPPs); late-stage legal, financial, engineering, procurement, construction, tariff, and environmental advisors; identification and due diligence on potential PPP partners; addressing gaps in regulatory regimes; shared costs on institutional/regulatory and commercial capacity; and speeding the ability to obtain site and water rights. Obtaining environmental permits and detailed environmental analysis for bid, as well as capacity of a country to increase the predictability of obtaining environmental permits was key.

INNOVATIVE FINANCE

Unlocking new sources of capital and lowering the higher perceived risk to developers is another catalytic use of U.S. development resources. A number of tools could buy down the costs of projects so that the end product, such as

---

42. See USAID's Africa Infrastructure Program (http://pdf.usaid.gov/pdf_docs/PDACP534.pdf), which has provided late-stage transactional support and regulatory/advisory services for about a dozen African country utilities, as well as private project developers. MCC's second compact in Ghana is also looking at capacity building to support a more enabling environment for specific U.S. power investors.
43. This discussion focuses primarily on the case of energy sector potential investments in Africa.

electricity or water, is less expensive to the ultimate consumer. For example, in MCC's water project in Jordan to increase the availability of water, viability gap funding was used to lower the cost to the poor and increase the number of beneficiaries that could benefit from the program.

More private actors would be willing to co-invest in and around U.S. development priorities if they could receive the right mix of guarantees and risk-sharing instruments provided by the U.S. government.[44, 45]

The challenge for U.S. agencies under a sustainable development paradigm is to develop new ways of sharing risk and catalyzing capital in developing sectors like energy and agriculture that support the success of existing projects, attract new investment, and help bring projects to scale.

U.S. agencies have found it difficult to use a full spectrum of government incentives that encourage private-sector investment—across both equity and debt instruments. However, the International Finance Corporation (IFC) and other Development Finance Institutions, such as PROPARCO, traditionally take equity positions in private projects and guarantee equity, particularly in high-risk sectors such as infrastructure.

While some agencies have the statutory authority to provide funding directly to private actors, Congress has sent mixed signals to agencies on the degree to which they can participate in funds,[46] for example, or guarantee equity, which holds the potential to mobilize considerable additional financing. Apart from OPIC funds, risk sharing with the private sector has been limited to debt instruments.

Agencies are nevertheless finding innovative ways, case-by-case, to engage non-aid actors to a greater extent. For example, USAID has taken a position as a limited partner equity investor in a project in Pakistan, through a grant agreement with a third party, and again, in India, as a limited partner, using a credit guarantee to provide equity-like resources through an institutional investor. USAID has also provided grants for technical assistance that have served to reduce the risk for a number of companies along agricultural supply chains of equity partners in Ghana. Reimbursable grants that lower equity requirements and provide some comfort for possible first losses are also being explored by agencies, along with risk capital funds, managed by third parties, that can be deployed to meet the specific needs of investors at arm's length.

Another way innovative finance tools could catalyze sustainable investment is by more aggressive and creative use of grant funding for guarantees. In the energy sector, for example, a significant constraint to investment is the fact that most countries that are energy project investment destinations are also under considerable IMF scrutiny to improve their balance sheets. Host-country government guarantees are frowned upon, even in sectors that are development priorities, and in the case of some countries, have been prohibited.

MCC compact funding and USAID's Development Credit Authority could play catalytic roles here by increasing the comfort of banks to guarantee projects at both the front and back end[47] of project development, where risks are highest.[48]

---

44. See Daniel F. Runde, *Sharing Risk in a World of Dangers and Opportunities: Strengthening U.S. Development Finance Capabilities* (Washington, DC: CSIS, December 2011), p. 22, http://csis.org/files/publication/111205__Runde_SharingRisk_Web.pdf.

45. Note that in 2012 OPIC, USTDA, and Ex-Im Bank announced a U.S.-Africa Clean Energy Development Finance Center (CEDFC) that will house a $20 million facility to help companies combine USTDA project planning and pre/post-feasibility with OPIC risk mitigation and Ex-Im Bank trade finance in the clean-energy sector.

46. Georgia proposed and successfully implemented under an MCC compact a Regional Development Fund, MCC's sole investment fund. Both debt and equity investments were made to 10 small and medium-sized enterprises (SMEs) engaged in a range of manufacturing and services, and returns have been largely positive. After the compact was implemented, congressional staff discouraged the use of MCC funds in this way.

47. For example, France's PROPARCO has successfully guaranteed project risk during the last five years of major infrastructure projects in Jordan.

48. The need for greater use of grant funding for first-loss guarantees by MCC and USAID has been noted, as has the need for greater use of equity, equity funds, and mezzanine financing to enhance the ability of a project to attract adequate debt financing and to provide patient and seed capital for sustainable projects and to encourage entrepreneurs. See Runde, *Sharing Risk in a World of Dangers and Opportunities*, pp., 6, 15, and 22.

Partial risk and partial credit guarantees could fill this gap, covering a range of risks, including coverage for lenders against the risk of a public entity like a utility not paying a project developer. Notably, changes to government regulatory and legal frameworks can also be covered with these instruments.

The African Development Bank and USAID are developing a Partial Risk Guarantee set-aside for power projects in Africa that will help fill this gap. The World Bank, the IFC, the African Trade Insurance Agency, and Multilateral Investment Guarantee Agency (MIGA) also provide them to some degree, but demand from potential investors, in the energy sector in particular, far exceeds what these development finance institutions can now deliver, and this demand is expected to increase. For example, projects that have not been previously approved by the World Bank do not qualify, and the application process is time and labor intensive, especially for small companies.

Capital guarantee funds guarantee the principal invested and increase the comfort level of institutions willing to invest equity in funds. These funds would be useful to attract new sources of capital, such as pension funds, to priority infrastructure. Pension funds represent an abundant source of capital for long-term investments, including private equity, infrastructure, and energy. However, pension funds remain largely untapped in Africa due to a combination of regulatory restrictions, capacity constraints, and the development of new financing products that would attract long-term investors to key sectors.[49]

Use of mezzanine funds, or debt capital that gives the lender the right to convert to equity, could be used more aggressively by U.S. agencies and significantly increase the ability of small businesses to get standard financing.

Use of crop insurance, or other ways of mitigating risk and providing long-term, patient capital for agriculture investors is a gap identified by companies.

Combining grant and investment instruments could help. Technical assistance is often the most effective risk-mitigation strategy, and it is most impactful when it is combined with funding. Currently OPIC does not have authority to provide technical assistance in combination with its finance, which could help address this gap. Coordinating packages that include capabilities across agencies, such as an MCC grant or OPIC loan with USAID technical support, could be the focus of future coordinative efforts, at the direction of the NSS or a delegated agency. OPIC and MCC country partners could tap USAID's technical assistance capability, but like the private sector, cannot always anticipate synching their needs to USAID mission budget cycles. Other donors, such as SNV of the Netherlands, successfully provide grants for technical assistance, often in combination with small amounts of patient capital. ▶

---

49. African investment bank BGL Group reported in 2010 that South Africa, Kenya, Ghana, Nigeria, Botswana, and Tanzania collectively had over $196 billion in pension fund assets.

CHAPTER 4
Reexamining Policy Restrictions

The issue of whether the U.S. development finance tool box is up to the task of implementing the vision of the Global Development Policy Directive, or specific initiatives, like Power Africa and Grow Africa, is also related to a handful of largely self-imposed policy restrictions that can limit the ability of agencies to more aggressively use tools that mitigate risk and lower the costs of investing in higher-risk countries and sectors.

Promoting sustainable investment in the power and agriculture sectors, on the one hand, while U.S. finance programs are sidelined by an array of restrictions that hamper their ability to support U.S. investors willing to make investments in those sectors, on the other, is inconsistent policy at best and undermines the ability of agencies to leverage U.S. development resources with non-aid actors. A reexamination of how these limitations could be modified by administration executive orders and other means in the near term, in consultation with congressional and stakeholder interests, could help rectify this inconsistency.

OPIC's carbon-emission cap and requirement and other restrictions that limit the agency's ability to play a substantial role in developmentally transformational sectors like energy and agriculture, could be reexamined. Companies interested in mitigating their investment risk with U.S. government tools, such as OPIC loan guarantees and insurance, would welcome a reexamination of OPIC's policy limit on the gas emissions potentially generated by the projects in its portfolio. The cap limits the agency's ability to finance any gas-related investment or even investments that could indirectly impact a country's carbon footprint, despite the mix of energy alternatives needed to implement both Power Africa and an ambitious policy on Climate Change. This is true particularly in the case of Power Africa countries like Nigeria, which will by necessity be heavily dependent on gas to meet their future electricity needs.

This limit is not statutorily mandated, but is considered restrictive by project developers at 100,000 particulates a year. Companies argue the cap has produced a chilling effect that discourages almost any energy-related proposal that could have a direct or indirect impact on total emissions.[50]

---

50. The Royce bill (H.R. 2548, 113th Congress, 1st session) reauthorizes OPIC for three years and seeks to help sub-Saharan African countries develop an appropriate mix of power solutions to increase access to electricity. This could be a vehicle to make an exception to the emissions cap to enable adequate financing for energy projects in sub-Saharan African countries. Another approach could be a Presidential Directive, with congressional and stakeholder consultation, to articulate a new policy that could facilitate projects that result in a net reduction of gas emissions—through the replacement of older coal-fired plants with new, more efficient technologies after an assessment, perhaps by the Council on Environmental Quality, in coordination with the Environmental Protection Agency and USAID.

A similar impediment is OPIC's requirement for a U.S. nexus. For a project to qualify for OPIC financing, there must be meaningful involvement of a U.S. entity, such as ownership by a U.S. citizen, or an entity with at least 25 percent U.S. equity. This has limited the ability of OPIC to, for example, provide insurance or other guarantees that would increase the comfort of investors in pension funds for infrastructure investment in Africa.

The Federal Credit Reform Act of 1990, which regulates how U.S. government credit programs (e.g., loan guarantees) are budgeted to help ensure U.S. budgets are adequate to cover defaults, does not address how to handle new instruments such as equity guarantees, crop insurance, and carbon credits. This limits the ability of the Office of Management and Budget to expansively interpret its regulatory authority in enforcing the Act, as well as the creative application of existing tools and new instruments by U.S. government agencies. The Act has never been reexamined, legislatively or by the administration, and lies under the jurisdiction of two budget committees. The administration could propose changes to Congress in how they might bring the Act up to date in light of a more relevant development model that seeks to attract and leverage private capital. ▶

CHAPTER 5
Conclusion

The question this paper has posed is whether the way we do development can keep up with the changing landscape brought about by the awareness of the business community that their growth is increasingly tied to their ability to play a more meaningful role in development.

Reorienting U.S. development strategy to realize a sustainable development model is indeed, as the 2010 Presidential Policy Directive notes, a long-term proposition. However, now that the vision has been properly set, experiments are underway, and lessons are being learned, the agenda is clear and achievable. The policy challenge now posed is to ensure U.S. development agency tools and institutional frameworks can become relevant to this new landscape, and meet the needs of partners willing to participate in its implementation.

Bringing U.S. government processes, tools, and incentives up to the task of achieving more sustainable development outcomes by going beyond partnerships to attract investment and engage the core business of companies is the next step. More aggressive and innovative development finance tools, targeted capacity building, an expanded project development table that includes potential investors, multi-stakeholder approaches, or contributing to corporate platforms where governments are not in the lead, were suggested as possibilities.

They imply a new role for government that is primarily catalytic. It is a role that proactively identifies and coordinates support for investors willing to take the higher risks of investing with development impact. It is a role that deploys development resources differently, and uses development finance tools more creatively, flexibly, and coherently. It is an approach that is less about reshaping interagency architecture and NSS-led processes and more about strategic use of what investors need to reevaluate the risk profile of projects in developmentally impactful sectors.

These steps, along with a reexamination of agency policy and statutory barriers that have made achieving the vision an uphill effort for agencies and companies to date, is an agenda for the administration to indeed harness all the tools at our disposal, especially the development impact of the private sector.

Purely government-to-government approaches are a less direct route to achieving the vision of attracting non-aid partners to U.S. development priorities for more sustainable outcomes. Finding the intersection between investors' interests and development goals is more likely when stimulating investment is the focus, rather than grafting private-sector interests into the development equation after project parameters are set.

Going forward, there is an opportunity for Partnership for Growth to evolve in this direction, along with other administration initiatives. There is nothing inconsistent between sustainable development and country-led approaches under Partnership for Growth, Power Africa, Feed the Future, or MCC compacts. Indeed, they can be completely reinforcing.

While the jury is still out on the success of a development model that makes sustainable growth the priority, this approach has great potential to concentrate U.S. agency reforms on what is most relevant to investors, changing the paradigm one project at a time.

Of equal importance to the success of this evolution will be greater responsibility on the part of a business community interested in being a more active partner in a private-sector-led U.S. trade and development strategy. Agencies will find it easier to be responsive and promote needed policy and statutory changes when their efforts are accompanied by greater congressional understanding of why these changes are so fundamental to the future effectiveness of U.S. trade and development strategy. Mixed signals from stakeholders have made operationalizing a new paradigm difficult to achieve. On the one hand, some members call for sustainable development solutions that cost less and leverage non-aid actors to a greater degree, while on the other, they resist the policy and legislative changes necessary to achieve those goals.

A strong business constituency willing to articulate why a new paradigm is needed that more effectively stimulates the economic growth that will create the next tier of markets for U.S. companies will be key, and can make a difference in determining whether the political environment in Congress will help or hinder this new vision. ▲

Appendix: Case Study
Notional Toolbox for Energy Investments in Africa

	Company Risks/Needs	Gaps	U.S. Government Tools/ Agencies	Other Development Finance Institutions
Project Development Axis	**Equity/grants** —Patient/seed capital and mezzanine finance[1]	U.S. government agencies do not guarantee equity; Patient/seed capital and mezzanine finance. Solutions: Reimbursable grants and use of grants (e.g., Millennium Challenge Corporation (MCC) compacts) to reduce equity requirements as equity substitute; Third-party grant agreements for use as equity funds and patient capital; risk capital funds	Overseas Private Investment Corporation (OPIC)—Africa Catalyst Fund (up to $100 million for SMEs pan-Africa); ManoCap Frontier Fund (multi-sector SME in West Africa). OPIC mezzanine fund but not for Africa. USAID—Sustainable Energy Fund for Africa trust fund, now accepting other donor contributions; challenge grants (e.g., PoweringAg); Grants of up to $300,000 for clean energy that empowers smallholders—up to $27 million total. $7.5 billion of MCC compacts and threshold programs in 39 countries.	African Development Bank (AfDB)—Africa50Fund to fill funding gaps in Africa's transport, power, water, and communications systems. Will raise $10 billion in equity to be leveraged to $100 billion in infrastructure projects with both project development and project finance business lines. International Finance Corporation (IFC)—equity-linked instruments; private equity funds; quasi-equity finance; will take 5-15% equity interest in projects without control; World Bank—Development Marketplace grants for innovative development through early-stage seed funding.
	Capacity building pre-feasibility: —Country Public-Private Partnership (PPP) capability —Negotiation of off-takes —Transaction advice for utilities to negotiate Power Purchase Agreement (PPAs) —Shared due diligence on regulatory regime —Environmental impact/permits —Site rights of way/water rights/etc. —Capacity to encourage country use of pension funds, perhaps through bond offerings as source of infrastructure finance.	Solution: Pre-feasibility country capacity and early project development risks related to country capacity that could be shared	USAID Africa Infrastructure Program (transactional, regulatory, and advisory support for countries/utilities); grants used as seed financing geared to technical assistance for initial start-up. —U.S. Trade and Development Agency (USTDA) grants for training for utilities, development of feed-in tariffs that support power generation and support choosing PPP partners; grants to support Independent Power Producer (IPP) market models and streamline regulatory functions for private-sector participation (e.g., grant to Nigerian utility to develop renewable IPP framework).	AfDB—Africa Guarantee Fund includes capacity building for SMEs, along with guarantees to financial institutions to stimulate financing to SMEs in Africa (co-funded with Spain and Denmark).

---

[1] Debt capital that gives the lender the right to convert to equity; treated like equity on a company's balance sheet, so it is easier for the SME to get standard financing.

	Feasibility	Bankable feasibility studies; Solution: MCC or USAID funding?	USTDA—desk/preliminary feasibility studies.	
	Post-feasibility: —Transaction advisers for RFPs and to structure PPPs —Late-stage legal, financial, engineering, procurement, construction, tariff, and environmental advisers —ID and due diligence PPP partners —Address gaps in regulatory regime —Permitting —Detailed Environmental Assessment for bid —Institutional/regulatory ad commercial strategies	Shared post-feasibility costs could accelerate and attract new investment, especially from smaller companies		
	Guarantees —First loss —Partial risk —Credit risk (breach of payment contract) —Termination	Flexible, accessible guarantees for projects that may not be World Bank approved. Solutions: —MCC grants for range of guarantees; - MCC/USAID reimbursable grants —MCC grants to purchase insurance from private companies for investors; —MCC guarantees for last years of project beyond OPIC 10-year tenors; —USAID grants as funds or guarantees to access pension funds —Using DCA as first loss for energy projects or as guarantees for local	USAID/AfDB set-aside for partial risk guarantees for power projects in Africa; risk capital funds that could be used for first loss. Development Credit Authority (DCA)—loan guarantees for banks; partial credit guarantees ExIm Bank—long-term loan guarantees for buyers of U.S. exports	World Bank—partial risk guarantees; IFC—partial credit guarantees; African Development Bank—Sustainable Energy for Africa Fund and Partial Risk Guarantees; also Africa Guarantee Fund (AFG) provides loan portfolio and financial guarantees to financial institutions to encourage lending to SMEs, along with capacity support for both banks and SMEs.

		bank credit for project development.		
	Insurance Political risk Credit risk Currency risk Crop insurance	Solutions: —Credit risk insurance to insure nonpayment by utilities; —MCC grants to purchase private insurance; —Risk mitigation product for agriculture.	OPIC currency inconvertibility	African Trade Insurance Agency (credit risk) Multilateral Investment Guarantee Agency (MIGA)—long-term political risk insurance to project sponsors, including sovereign nonpayment ($180 million maximum)
	Long-term debt financing	—No OPIC financing for gas-related projects (carbon caps); —OPIC tenor for last 5 years of project?	OPIC—Up to $5 billion committed to financing and insuring energy projects. —SME and structured financing ($350,000–$250 million) up to 10 years. OPIC/USTDA/ExIm Clean Energy Development and Finance Center (CEDFC) $20 million facility combining USTDA project planning and pre/post-feasibility with OPIC risk mitigation with ExIm trade finance; ExIm—fixed-rate loans directly to foreign buyers of U.S. equipment or services and for exporters involved in large-scale infrastructure projects.	AfDB—$1.65 billion committed in energy infrastructure for next 5 years.
	Technical assistance	—Ability to access technical assistance quickly and flexibly for specific projects; —Ability to combine technical assistance with debt finance to lower risk.	—USAID: $285 million in technical assistance, grants and risk mitigation to advance private-sector energy transactions and help SSA governments adopt and implement policy, regulatory and enabling environment reforms necessary to attract investment in the power sector. —USTDA: project development; —Training grants for distribution companies to learn how to reduce power losses; —Grants for studies to convert gas to electricity —OPIC/USTDA CEDFC $20 million facility, technical assistance for projects	

Policy/regulatory	Transaction specific	USAID: $285 million in technical-assistance, grants, and risk mitigation to support policy, regulatory, and enabling environmental reforms needed to attract investment.	
		USTDA: technical assistance that supports policy/regulatory reform related to infrastructure development;	
Trade/project finance		U.S.-Africa Clean Energy Development and Finance Center (Johannesburg, South Africa) to assist sub-Saharan African energy developers implement clean-energy projects.	
		OPIC: limited recourse project finance	
		Ex-Im Bank:	
		Short-term Africa Initiative: financing for African infrastructure-related transactions.	
		—Commercial guarantees for medium/long-term loans by banks to African buyers;	
		—Working capital guarantees for U.S. exporters;	
		—Export credit insurance;	
		—Project financing for most African countries.	
Market linkages		USTDA reverse-trade missions for African buyers of U.S. products (e.g., funding of African energy companies to come to United States to learn about gas storage; procurement training for foreign purchasers)	
		U.S. Department of Commerce/State trade/policy missions	

About the Author

Jeri Jensen is a senior associate with the CSIS Project on U.S. Leadership in Development. She is also the founder of Business Driven Development, LLC, a strategic advisory firm that increases social investment in developing countries by enhancing the development impact of the core businesses of international investors and enabling donors to leverage their participation in economic development with the private sector.

Ms. Jensen's 30 years of experience includes serving as vice president at the Initiative for Global Development, a network of CEOs and senior executives interested in strategic investment in Africa, and managing director for private-sector initiatives at the Millennium Challenge Corporation, a major U.S. donor to developing countries. She has also worked as deputy assistant U.S. trade representative for Southeast Asia and for labor affairs. As executive director for trade policy and promotion at the U.S. Department of Commerce, she managed coordination of trade-promotion efforts across all U.S. trade, finance, and investment agencies. She also led trade and economic strategy for Latin America at the National Security Council and was a strategic adviser to the chairman of the U.S. Export-Import Bank. She holds a Master of Science in foreign service from Georgetown University and a Bachelor of Arts in political science from Northwestern University.